Join the SPIN Corps!

By Wally Satzewich
and Roxanne Christensen

www.spinfarming.com

SPIN

MB McBurgers

SPIN-Farming
Workshop
Saturday

MB McBurgers

I0067171

A guide to using SPIN-Farming® to teach the business of growing food.

ISBN: 978-0-615-65076-0

What this book provides: how-to sub-acre farming information.
What this book does NOT provide: legal, accounting or professional business advice or services.

For information on licensing, foreign or domestic rights, or bulk copy orders for educational use, contact Roxanne Christensen at rchristensen@infocommercegroup.com, or at 610-505-9189.

Meet A Few SPIN Corps Members...

Here are some of your fellow SPIN farmers who are growing education and opportunities for others.

Biodynamic SPIN farmer Linda Borghi
Walker Valley, NY

Linda is the owner/operator of Abundant Life Farm in Walker Valley, NY. Her recipe for this half-acre farm is equal parts SPIN-Farming, biodynamics and lasagna gardening. Carved out of a wooded hillside, the farm was up and operational in 6 months. Though records are not yet kept on how quickly farms can be created, this must be some sort of record. It is also the third location for her farm and proves just how portable the farming profession can be. Linda's sales channels include restaurants, a 15 member CSA and mobile farm stand.

Linda has worked both sides of the fence, as a vendor and producer. She began her career in 1977, managing 4 star restaurants on the upper east side of New York, including La Grenouille, Bruno's, Toscana and Piccolo Mondo. She began farming in 1988 on Block Island, RI where she first established Abundant Life Farm. There she invented a 5 gallon pasteurization machine, and was the only farm in the country with a "herd" of one cow to be licensed to sell cheese to the public. In 1996 she returned to the mainland to manage the cut flower operation of 26 Costco wholesale locations, from Norfolk, VA to Holbrook, Long Island. In 1998 she was the first intern at the Pfeiffer Center Garden in Chestnut Ridge NY, which pioneered the practices of Rudolf Steiner's biodynamic agriculture.

In 2004 she re-established Abundant Life Farm in Middletown, NY. In 2006 she began practicing SPIN-Farming. In 2007 Orange Magazine named her "Who's Who of Manure", and she opened the Eat Local Virtual Farm stand which created a direct distribution channel from farmer to eater. In 2008 she moved Abundant Life Farm to Walker Valley, NY. In 2009 Linda spoke at the United Nations at a conference entitled "Food, Famine and the Future of Food Technology."

Linda takes farming to the guy and gal in the street so they can take safe, healthy and nutritious foods to their families, neighbors and communities!

Green industry veteran SPIN farmer Lee McBride, Huntsville, AL

Lee's 32 year career has spanned landscape management, tree care, organic lawn maintenance and edible landscaping, so SPIN-Farming was the natural next step for him. Teaching comes naturally to him, too. Whether in his own businesses or through advocacy groups and nonprofits, he has always shared his horticultural knowledge with employees, prospective Master Gardeners, community volunteers and families.

Lee is a consulting Arborist who specializes in the diagnosis and management of tree diseases and disorders and the protection of trees during construction, But his dedication to all things green has led him to serve as council member of the Alabama Urban Forestry Association; volunteer Arborist for the City of Madison Beautification and Tree Board; chair of the education committee of the North Alabama Food Policy Council; and adviser to the Greene Street Farmers Market. Lee serves on the board of Care Assurance System for the Aging (CASA), and its garden committee, and can usually be found at the CASA garden every Saturday morning.

In 2006 Lee found SPIN-Farming which was the impetus for his garden coaching and farm mentoring career. After implementing the methods slowly, over time, at the CASA garden and proving the concepts, Lee believes SPIN is the one method that can feed people and create economic opportunity all over the south.

As an adviser to a new non-profit incubator farm in Huntsville which trains farmers in the production and selling of high quality produce using shared equipment and resources, Lee is demonstrating and developing southern-style SPIN, and he can't wait to you show y'all how it's done. Can razorback purple hull peas be a high-value crop? He'll let you know...

Lee has a pretty sophisticated approach to SPIN-Farming. It might be his landscaping background. He thinks that the next great American landscape may very well be defined by hundreds of thousands of working, productive sub-acre farms. But he knows it is not just about aesthetics. It will be the manifestation of a whole new value system.

Meet A Few SPIN Corps Members…

Here are some of your fellow SPIN farmers who are growing education and opportunities for others.

Seeker, teacher and SPIN farmer Mark Voss
Madison, WI

Mark found his calling in Africa. There, by the light of a kerosene lamp, he discovered the work of Wendell Berry, Wes Jackson and Helen and Scott Nearing, while by day he labored as a Peace Corps volunteer with the subsistence farmers in the Togo bush. Later he made a pilgrimage to meet one of his agro-heroes, Masanobu Fukuoka, on the island of Shikoku, Japan. A natural seeker, Mark also studied biodynamics with Ruth and Dick Zinniker. He found his way to SPIN-Farming out of necessity.

With several apprenticeships under his belt but little money for large acreage and equipment, Mark first rented land in 1993, then purchased a home with a large lot and resolved to become an urban farmer. That was pre-SPIN-Farming, and his success has been hard won. That's why he places SPIN-Farming right up there with all the big farming gurus. "It codifies a body of experience that many have been engaged in for years," he says, so it makes it much easier for new farmers to get started and more likely they will succeed.

His farm business, Voss Organics, encompasses a 400 square foot backyard hoophouse and 3,000 square feet of certified organic raised beds on a city lot, as well as 3 of his neighbors backyards, where he is pushing the limits of SPIN's revenue benchmarks. His markets include 2 farmers markets, and premier food cooperatives and restaurants. Mark, who also holds a BA in economics from the University of Illinois and is an educator of adults and children, is using SPIN-Farming to not only farm, but to provide training for those who want to farm in a new way, combining the insights of the gurus with the practicalities of sub-acre farming.

In spite of his deep appreciation for indigenous practices, Mark has a very modern perspective on farming. He realizes that to attract new generations to farming, they need to be appealed to, not with romantic ideas of how the world used to be, but rather in a way that takes advantage of all the knowledge accumulated to date and reflects current cultural contexts.

Blue Ribbon SPIN farmer John Sealander
Franklin, NC

It is a cliche: most farmers are great at growing, but failures at properly valuing and selling their crops. As a result they barely eke out a living. This is one farming tradition that SPIN-Farming seeks to change, and John Sealander is just the SPIN farmer to help.

John lived his entire adult life as a straight commissioned salesman. In 24 months he went from having never farmed a day in his life to being the "Famous Amos" of free range chickens in Macon County, NC, selling $4 eggs in a $2 market. He won blue ribbons two years in a row at the county fair, and his Blue Ribbon Eggs brand now dominates the local market. But the labor of a poultry operation outweighed the return, and that led John to SPIN-Farming.

What sold him is that SPIN-Farming brings organic farming out of the mystical clouds and into the everyday world of ordinary people and the market place. It's a pure production, processing and marketing system for occupational farmers. Not theoretical, not speculative and not philosophical. Real, both in work and in profit. So now, on a 1,000 sq. ft. planting of spinach John can earn up to $4,100 on a $30 seed purchase, some bags and delivery costs.

But he watches fellow farmers work terrifically hard all week only to put their lettuce on the table and then sell themselves short, or not at all. John's attitude is you can buy cheap, or buy good, but not both. He uses what he calls the "Integrity Sell" to match the features of his products with the values of his customers. He uses SPIN to turn a greens business into greenbacks.

John is your typical SPIN farmer, which is to say there is nothing typical about him. He took the long and winding road to farming. Now that he's where he wants to be in his career, he's using SPIN-Farming to help others complete their journeys. He has valuable knowledge of the ways of nature and persuasion. There isn't a better representative of the type of farming that SPIN stands for, which is entrepreneurial in spirit and community-based.

Meet A Few SPIN Corps Members...

Here are some of your fellow SPIN farmers who are growing education and opportunities for others.

SPIN-based community development pioneer Jody Veler
Medford, NJ

Jody has years of experience in developing a wide variety of community agricultural programs and using them to drive economic development. She earned her SPIN stripes in urban areas by overcoming the challenges unique to nonprofit and community-based organizations including fundraising, coalition building, volunteer management, conflict resolution, training, land access and control and soil remediation. In 2008 she established the first SPIN-Farming-based cooperative on public property in collaboration with a county government. Hiring, training and overseeing multicultural workers and staff, Jody built an operation that supported a 100 member CSA in its first year.

A former Sergeant with the Trenton Department of Corrections, Jody began her second career in agriculture as a volunteer for AmeriCorps, providing horticulture therapy to adults with brain injuries, and training at-risk youth in greenhouse production. She has also developed a wide variety of farming skills through formal agricultural studies, including Integrated Pest Management (IPM) Scout, and seasonal positions including Horticultural Therapist, Fruit Tree Research Assistant, and Viticulture Assistant.

Jody received her Master's degree in Community Economic Development from Southern New Hampshire University in 2008. Currently she is developing a nonprofit incubator program to assist small and emerging nonprofit organizations to build their capacity.

Jody has seen that entrepreneurialism can and does occur anywhere. She does not do charity work. The only gifts she bestows are tools for self-actualization and self determination.

SPIN farmer and master of many trades Ed Garrett
Davis, CA

Why would an agriculturalist with 30+ years experience, multiple degrees (latest is a BS from UC Davis in International Agriculture Development), a career that combined successful and profitable self-employment mixed with semi-conventional employment, and a resume 6 pages long want to teach SPIN-Farming? Because SPIN-Farming does not pretend that the economics of farming are the same as they ever were. Because it is based on meeting the growing demand for local food from urban and suburban markets. Because it turns urbanization to the farmer's advantage. Because it allows people, at any stage of life, to start a farm of their own by serving the land and their customers instead of debt. Because it is attracting a broad mix of people, reflecting America's increasing diversity. Because it works.

Ed is in a good position to know. His professional experience has covered a lot of bases. Large farm manager. Livestock Auction Director. State Fair Executive. Agricultural Lab Technician. Property and Business Developer for an organic truck farm, organic medicinal herb grower and a commercial rhizome producer. Sheep Groomer. Construction Manager. Basic Electrical Repair and Woodworking Instructor. Soil and Plant Science Tutor. Sacramento Examiner Blogger. Small farm Owner.

Where it is all coming together is at his 4.5 acre Fresh Spin Farms in Davis, CA where Ed is using SPIN to create a working farm, education center and base camp for food initiatives with the local food bank and Farm to School program.

Over his years of experience Ed has seen a lot of what works, as well as what needs to change. The planet and people have always been part of farming's triple bottom line, but what has been missing for too long is profit. Ed is now spreading the word on SPIN-Farming because he has seen how it can be used to start an income-producing farm quickly and efficiently.

Join the SPIN Corps...

The SPIN Corps is Ready to Welcome You. 13

SECTION 1: What You Are Joining. 16

Purpose 16

Your Responsibilities 17

Qualifications 17

Standard Operating Equipment 17

The Story of SPIN-Farming's Developer, Wally Satzewich. 18

Wally Meets Roxanne 19

SECTION 2: Your Marching Orders 22

Get In Step. 22

Marching Order #1: Communicate what makes SPIN-Farming different. 22

Questions to answer. 23

Resources. 24

Exercises 24

Marching Order #2: Understand and communicate SPIN-Farming's key concepts. 25

Questions to answer. 25

Resources. 25

Exercises 25

Marching Order #3: Turn intentions into action: the SPIN-Farming land base 26

Questions to answer. 27

Resources. 27

Exercises 27

Marching Order #4: Get farmers producing 28

Questions to answer. 29

Resources. 29

Exercises 29

Marching order #5: Make farmers efficient with work flow management 30

Questions to answer. 30

Resources. 30

Exercise 30

Marching order #6: Help farmers turn harvesting into a five-days-a-week practice 30

Questions to answer. 31

Resources. 31

Exercises 31

Marching order #7: Get farmers started affordably with SPIN's signature investments. 31

Questions to answer. 33

Resources. 33

Exercises 33

Marching order #8: Sell farmers on direct marketing and innovative pricing. 34

Questions to answer. 35

Resources. 35

Exercises 35

SECTION 3: How You Make Money. 39

Serving a need. 39

Promoting yourself. 39

Product #1: SPIN-Farming Guides 40

Product #2: SPIN-Farming Workshops. 40

Product # 3: SPIN-Farming Online Support 41

Special Bonus – Good Times and Fellowship 41

Are You Ready?. 42

Looking Ahead 42

Lexicon

Frequently Asked Questions

About the Authors

BORN
TO BE
USED

...to answer this question »

How can I become more involved with the SPIN-Farming organization?

Welcome!

When we began hearing the question "How can I become more involved with the SPIN-Farming organization?" several times a week, we realized that SPIN-Farming had become more than just a new way to farm. When we pressed further about their ambitions, people told us that governments and non-profits have too much on their plates right now, and there are limits to what well-intentioned individuals and households can do.

To create a world that feeds itself more healthfully and less destructively, what they see is needed is the kind of effort that is more impactful than what the individual can do, and less grandiose than what is attempted by established institutions. Against a backdrop of dramatically changing economics, people want to use SPIN-Farming as a rallying point to build local food capacity by creating more neighborhood-based, income-producing farms. They want to inspire, teach and mentor others like themselves, and earn money doing it.

What they see SPIN-Farming providing is:

- a non-technical farming system that can be implemented by those with no farming experience or any prior connection to the land
- a concept that is easily understood
- a brand that both growers and consumers want to support
- products that move people from talk to action
- a way to jump start their own business, or expand or diversify an existing one

If you, like them, want to be part of an expanding, exuberant people-to-people experiment, the SPIN Corps is ready to welcome you. »

Help the explosive hodge podge of new farming activity realize its full potential. »

Join the SPIN Corps!

Section 1: What You Are Joining

Purpose…Your responsibilities…Qualifications…Standard
operating equipment…The story of SPIN's developer, Wally
Satzewich…Wally meets Roxanne…This is where you enter the
story…

Section 2: Your Marching Orders
Section 3: How You Make Money

PEOPLE AROUND THE WORLD are pioneering a new way to farm. It is sub-acre in scale and entrepreneurial in spirit. It is unencumbered by dogma and grounded in local communities. It requires minimal infrastructure so it's easy on the pocketbook. It's organic-based, so it's easy on the environment. Those who practice it are showing how to make more from less. Those who support it are accelerating the shift back to locally-based food production. The SPIN Corps is your opportunity to teach the type of farming anyone can understand and more and more want to practice...

SECTION 1: What You Are Joining

Purpose

In a world that is finally facing up to the challenges of finite resources and dramatically changing economics, a corps of unlikely activists are, quite literally, taking matters into their own hands by taking up SPIN-Farming. SPIN stands for S-mall P-lot IN-tensive, and it is giving rise to a new class of non-traditional farmers who span geography, generations, income and social status.

What makes SPIN-Farming uniquely suited to the non-traditional farmer is that it is primarily a business model, one that makes it possible to generate significant income from sub-acre (less than an acre in size) land bases. With SPIN, farmers do not need much land to start their commercial operations. More importantly, they don't need to own any land at all; they can affordably rent or even barter their land base from neighbors, friends and relatives.

SPIN also greatly reduces the need for capital. Minimal infrastructure, reliance on hand labor to accomplish most farming tasks, utilization of existing water sources to meet irrigation needs, and situating close to markets all keep investment and overhead costs low. SPIN therefore removes the 2 big barriers to entry for new farmers – they don't need a lot of land or money.

By re-casting farming as a small business, these non-traditional farmers are making food production visible and palpable and galvanizing their communities around an activity that delivers both economic and environmental benefits. The SPIN Corps is a way to help this explosive hodge podge of new farming activity realize its full potential by providing a continual feedback loop of learning, experimentation and encouragement that is based on the entrepreneurial talent in local communities rather than on government or charitable support. It is easy to help people grow food. It is quite different to equip them with the ability to produce consistently, in significant volume, at commercial grade. That is the purpose of the SPIN Corps – to professionalize an endeavor that up until now has been fragmented, unorganized and unrecognized.

Your Responsibilities

As a SPIN Corps member you will:

- train and mentor new and established SPIN farmers via workshops and field days
- help groups whose mission is rebuilding local food systems incorporate SPIN-Farming training into their programs
- provide ongoing support and education to help SPIN farmers develop professionally
- create a SPIN-Farming demonstration site, which can be your farm
- represent SPIN-Farming at trade shows and local community events
- participate in the SPIN-Farming online email support group
- contribute photos to the SPIN online gallery and for use in SPIN publications
- help SPIN-Farming evolve by offering improvements to the system and conceptualizing new SPIN-centric product ideas

Qualifications

What you need to bring to the position of SPIN Corps member is:

- at least one season of generating income using the SPIN-Farming system
- familiarity with the Internet and email
- good communication skills
- the ability to teach the SPIN-Farming system

Standard Operating Equipment

Beginning with this guide, we'll equip you with all the knowledge and goodwill we've collected in our 6+ years in the field. Once you are formally accepted into the corps program you will also receive:

- detailed learning modules and photos you can use as a base for your SPIN workshop presentation
- collateral presentation and sales material including photos, Power Points, talking points, and pdf copies of handouts
- tips and resources for marketing SPIN guides and trainings

> It is easy to help people grow food. It is quite different to equip them with the ability to produce consistently, in significant volume, at commercial grade.

…a sub-acre farmer could earn as much, or more, income as a large scale operation, but with a lot less stress and overhead, and with more control over the operation, and with more certainty of success from year to year.

As added support, you'll get free membership in the SPIN Corps email group that acts as a brain trust and serves as an online collaborative mechanism for practicing SPIN Corps members around the world to ask and offer advice and share collective experiences. As a group member you can communicate with the other SPIN Corps members using a single email address. You can ask questions, strategize and pass on knowledge and resources that are emailed to everyone in the group, and group members respond if they have something to say.

While the SPIN Corps' mission is to help create the farmers of the future, its origin traces back to a Canadian farmer who, when others told him to get bigger or go home, went home. Read on to learn about SPIN-Farming's roots.

The Story of SPIN-Farming's Developer, Wally Satzewich

Wally did not come from a farm family. In 1981, he was driving a taxi and wondering what to do with his life. He began growing in his backyard in Saskatoon, Saskatchewan, a city of about 220,000, and selling at the Saskatoon Farmers Market, and that sealed his fate. He realized he was a farmer.

Like most farmers back then, he thought that in order to become successful, he needed more land. So he acquired 160 acres outside of Saskatoon along the Saskatchewan River where he started farming 20 acres, invested in an expensive irrigation system and brought in outside work crews. But he continued to live in Saskatoon and grow in his small yard there. Over time he realized he was growing high-value crops, like carrots, spinach and lettuce, in his small backyard, while growing low-value crops, like potatoes and onions, on his larger acreage in the country.

This distinction between a high-value and low-value crop made him realize the other advantages to city-based sub-acre farming. He could grow high-value crops in the city because he was not losing them to pests, such as deer and large scale insect infestations. He had the micro climate advantage in the city which allowed him to get to market much sooner and produce much later in the season. His irrigation system in the city was the water faucet - he did not have to depend on fluctuating river levels or worry about water quality.

His work crew in the city was he and his wife – he did not have to depend on outside labor. And looking at the numbers is what really made his head spin. Because what he saw was that even though the land base and overhead of sub-acre farming are a fraction of that of a large-scale farm, the bottom lines were similar. He realized that a sub-acre farmer could earn as much, or more, income as a large scale operator, but with a lot less stress and overhead, and with more control over the operation, and with more certainty of success from year to year. So instead of expanding his rural site, Futility Farm as he called it, Wally sold off all his acreage in the country, and he became a backyard urban farmer.

Wally Meets Roxanne

Like most modern collaborations, it was the Internet that brought them together. Roxanne Christensen was helping to start a project to prove the economic feasibility of urban farming in Philadelphia, PA, and Wally had the numbers. Or the number. $50,000. Gross. From a half-acre.

What, are you crazy? They heard that a lot. But an intrepid city employee at the Philadelphia Water Department, Nancy Weissman, was a sucker for long shots. She said, "Let's show'em." So in 2003 a half-acre SPIN demonstration farm was created on land operated by the Philadelphia Water Department under Wally's long distance guidance. The pilot project was meant to last 5 years, and it had one goal – to prove that an urban farm could generate $50,000 in gross sales from 20,000 square feet. It surpassed that goal in year 3, and with the use of season extension in year 4 it generated $68,000 gross.

Wally never doubted. He knew how effective a systemized approach to farming could be. And while he also knew that farming was "experiential", and that farmers learned from other farmers, he also knew that if the only way aspiring farmers could launch their careers was by trailing him around in his backyard plots, it would get pretty crowded up there in Saskatoon. What he needed was to document the system in some way. It so happened that Roxanne was a writer and, like Wally, had an entrepreneurial spirit. So together they wrote and produced the SPIN-Farming online learning series.

Launched in March of 2006, it is now being used by thousands of new farmers to get started – and stay - in business. Most, like Wally, do not come from traditional farm families. That may be why they appreciate SPIN's systematic approach and can make it work. It makes it easier to get started by eliminating the routine trial and error, providing benchmarks to gauge progress and keeping farmers focused on what matters most to their success. But farming is as much an art as a science. It takes lots of patience and humility, two things that are real luxuries today. And it takes ongoing support and knowledge and gear.

This is where you enter the story...

> What he needed was to document the system in some way.

Teach the type of farming anyone can understand and more and more want to practice. »

Join the SPIN Corps!

Section 1: What You Are Joining

Section 2: Your Marching Orders

Get In Step…Communicate what makes SPIN different…
Understand and communicate SPIN-Farming's key concepts…
Turn intentions into action: the SPIN-Farming land base…Get
farmers producing…Make farmers efficient with work flow
management…Help farmers turn harvesting into a five-day-a
week practice…Get farmers started affordably with SPIN's
signature investments…Sell farmers on direct marketing and
innovative pricing

Section 3: How You Make Money

What is novel about SPIN-Farming is that it is primarily a business model that makes sub-acre commercial production possible.

SECTION 2: Your Marching Orders

Get In Step

Each SPIN Corps member is one of a kind, but all of a type. They are all passionate about relocalizing food production and committed to the goal of recruiting and supporting new career farmers. But each one brings his or her own unique background, experience, style, perspective and capabilities to the corps.

To get you in step with other corps members, the following pages summarize what we feel is important to know about SPIN-Farming. We understand that each SPIN farmer adapts the system to his or her markets and climate, but these are the basic concepts and practices that define SPIN no matter where it takes root. Reading and understanding the material in this guide and going through the exercises are the best way we know to prepare you for what it takes to be an effective representative for SPIN-Farming. So here are your marching orders.

1. Communicate what makes SPIN different
2. Understand and communicate SPIN's key concepts
3. Turn intentions into action: the SPIN land base
4. Get farmers producing
5. Make farmers efficient with work flow management
6. Help farmers turn harvesting into a five-day-a-week practice
7. Get farmers started affordably with SPIN's signature investments
8. Sell farmers on direct marketing and innovative pricing

Marching Order #1:

Communicate what makes SPIN-Farming different

Your most important task as a SPIN Corps member is to help both aspiring farmers and the public understand why SPIN-Farming is different. While it is "small scale", there is nothing new about small scale farming. While it is organic-based, there is nothing new about organics. While it is intensive, other growing techniques produce lots of food.

What is novel about SPIN-Farming is that it is primarily a business model that makes sub-acre commercial production possible. Other farming systems are based on acres of production and focus primarily, if not exclusively, on agricultural practices. SPIN, however, emphasizes the business aspects and provides a financial and management system for having the business drive the agriculture, rather than the other way around. The advantages to following a farm start-up system are:

- it greatly reduces development time
- it eliminates much trial and error
- it shortens the learning curve
- it provides specific benchmarks to measure success
- it provides more control over outcomes and income
- it keeps the focus on what matters most to success
- it makes collaboration easier

While SPIN-Farming removes the 2 big barriers to entry – land and capital – it is also trying to remove a psychological one.

While SPIN-Farming removes the 2 big barriers to entry – land and capital – it is also trying to remove a psychological one. To "outsiders", the profession seems almost tribal. By providing a nontechnical and easy-to-implement system, SPIN opens up farming as a career to literally anyone, anywhere, and makes it less mysterious and intimidating.

Develop your own ideas on what makes SPIN different, and we will give you ours once you become accepted into the SPIN Corps program.

Questions to answer:

1. What are some compelling environmental, economic, political and social reasons to re-orient the current food production system towards one that is more locally-based?
2. In 100 words or less, how would you define SPIN-Farming?
3. What are the advantages to SPIN-Farming?
4. How can SPIN-Farming be used to recreate locally-based food systems?

Resources

SPIN-Farming® Basics – guide #1

SPIN-Farming website – www.spinfarming.com

Books:

Eat Here: Reclaiming Homegrown Pleasures in a Global Supermarket – Brian Halweil, Norton/WorldWatch Books

Animal, Vegetable, Miracle – Barbara Kingsolver, Harper

The Omnivore's Dilemma: A Natural History of Four Meals – Michael Pollan, Penguin Press

In Defense of Food: An Eater's Manifesto – Michael Pollan, Penguin Press

Food and the City: Urban Agriculture and the New Food Revolution – Jennifer Cockrell-King, Promethesus Books

The Urban Food Revolution: Changing the Way We Feed Cities – Peter Ladner, New Society Publishers

Breaking Through Concrete – David Hanson and Edwin Marty, University of California Press

Films:

Food Inc.

The Future of Food

King Corn

Exercises:

❏ Find your own sources of information on the local food movement, both online and in print

❏ Build a case for why it is worthwhile to re-establish locally-based commercial farms and food businesses

Marching Order #2:

Understand and communicate SPIN-Farming's key concepts

Your primary task as a SPIN Corps member is to help aspiring farmers develop a sub-acre mindset which requires them to think differently and even talk differently than the traditional farmer. The SPIN-Farming lexicon helps to develop this sub-acre farming mindset, and once you understand it and get comfortable using its terms, you will be well on your way to being an effective corps member. The point is to show the connection between knowing and using the terms in the lexicon and creating and running a high-income producing farm. You'll find the lexicon at the end of this guide. You will be using it a lot in your presentations and appearances.

The SPIN-Farming lexicon helps to develop the sub-acre farming mindset...

Questions to answer:

1. What are the key terms in the SPIN-Farming lexicon, and what do they mean?
2. How do SPIN-Farming's key terms work together to produce a framework for starting and operating a farming operation?
3. How does relay cropping increase production?
4. What kinds of crops would you recommend growing and why?
5. Why is high-road harvesting important?
6. What is the purpose of the 1-2-3 layout?

Resources

SPIN-Farming® Basics – guide #4 Key Concepts

SPIN-Farming website – www.spinfarming.com

Farmer's markets

Seed catalogs

Exercises:

❏ Develop examples of intensive relays and bi-relays
❏ Create a basic SPIN-Farming demo plot
❏ Document how you have implemented SPIN-Farming and the revenue you have achieved

You will encourage aspiring SPIN farmers to be flexible and resourceful in assembling a land base.

Marching Order #3:

Turn intentions into action: the SPIN-Farming land base

As a SPIN Corps member, you will help people view the world through SPIN glasses. When you put on SPIN glasses you start to see underutilized urban and peri-urban spaces, and pretty soon you start to see potential farms everywhere. But sometimes hurdles exist that prevent productive land use, and farming in cities in towns comes with some special considerations. Zoning is perhaps the biggest issue, and many municipalities are now reviewing their regulations to make them more farm-friendly. You should familiarize yourself with the current zoning regulations regarding commercial agriculture in your area and identify the governmental agencies that farmers can work with, or at least be aware of.

Another consideration is soil contamination, especially heavy metals, and soil fertility. Soil tests are always recommended. Identify all the hurdles and suggested strategies to deal with them. In this regard, networking among neighbors and government officials is extremely important. You do not need to become a soil expert yourself, but rather recommend the local agricultural, environmental and governmental groups whose expertise can be enlisted.

You will encourage aspiring SPIN farmers to be flexible and resourceful in assembling a land base. Some may start in their own backyards, or the yards of relatives, friends and neighbors, using SPIN's multi-locational approach. You should also encourage them to think expansively by using as much of their outdoor space as possible including fence lines, rooftops, container gardens on patios and driveways and alleys. When they have maxed out their outdoor space, they can use indoor space such as a spare bedroom, den or basement for starting transplants and shoot production. Once they have maxed out their own space, they can expand to neighboring yards or to a community garden plot, or to a larger peri-urban site.

Other land base options include public or private land surrounding schools, firehouses, hospitals, government offices and workplaces. Many apartment dwellers don't have yard space, so yard sharing and community garden plot rental are options for them. Renters can advertise for backyard or front lawn cropland online. Online resources for matching up aspiring famers and yard owners now exist in many areas. Roofs and indoor production are also options.

To promote commercial urban agriculture, some cities are beginning to develop land banks, and perhaps your city or town can be encouraged to do the same. Since most new farmers will be scouting out cropland amid concrete, you'll need to help them evaluate farm sites. Considerations for yardsharing agreements and criteria for evaluating a site's farming potential will be provided to you when you are accepted into the SPIN Corps.

The point is to help people realize what is possible and do what is practical when assembling a land base. And it is here that the advantage of the sub-acre scale is most apparent for a beginning farmer, because he or she can get started without taking on a crushing debt burden to purchase sizeable acreage. Another important point to understand is that if a novice farmer cannot master production on a sub-acre plot, their chances of success would not be increased by having even more land and overhead to manage. In fact, the advantage to SPIN that many miss is that it can increase the survival rate of new farmers who, might otherwise be undermined by pursuing the traditional approach. Those who give up might otherwise have succeeded if they weren't initially overburdened financially by debt and operationally by large acreage and overhead.

the advantage to SPIN that many miss is that it can increase the survival rate of new farmers…

Questions to answer:

1. If someone without a yard wants to do SPIN-Farming, what would you tell them?
2. How would you advise someone who is concerned about contaminated soil or heavy metals?
3. What is a multi-locational farm?
4. What mechanisms can be used to link individuals or groups with available land?

Resources

SPIN-Farming® Basics – guide #2, Getting Started

Digging Deeper #2, The Multi-locational Urban/Peri-urban Farm (in the SPIN-Farming online learning series)

Extension services and university agriculture departments

Garden clubs

Online listing sources such as Craigslist to connect landowners with aspiring farmers gardeners

Exercises:

❑ Describe the land base you are using for SPIN-Farming
❑ Take an inventory of parcels in and around your neighborhood or town that would be appropriate for farming, and list the reasons why
❑ Research local zoning regulations regarding commercial agriculture
❑ Identify any existing options farmers can use for finding land
❑ Find out about local soil contamination concerns and experiences
❑ Develop local resources and recommendations for dealing with soil contamination

It should be emphasized that SPIN is a production system not a belief system.

Marching Order #4:

Get farmers producing

SPIN-Farming encourages a wide variety of techniques, from rototillers to hand work, from containers, to raised beds. It should be emphasized that SPIN is a production system not a belief system. It is not predicated on any one method of soil prep or maintenance, and it does not advocate any one set of life principals or philosophy. It can be combined with biointensive, biodynamic, permaculture, vermaculture, acquaponics, double dig, no till. We recommend the use of a rototiller because it increases efficiency. But if a rototiller does not fit in with the way someone thinks the world should work, and they are willing to accept the possible consequences of decreased productivity, they can choose not to use it. SPIN's guiding principles are practicality and flexibility. Many farmers lock themselves into following just one method and often end up with poorly performing operations as a result. As a SPIN Corps member, you will encourage people to take as much from the SPIN-Farming system as makes sense to them and combine it with whatever other growing approaches they favor.

Here are the SPIN-Farming practices that you as a SPIN Corps member need to understand and explain.

Bed size and prep – Know the advantages of a standard size bed and different methods for prepping beds for planting.

Bed layout – Know how to use the 1-2-3 farm layout to allocate a land base to different areas of cropping intensity.

Fertility – Know that SPIN is organic-based to eliminate negative consequences to the environment and minimize expense. Different fertilizing strategies can be used for different plots, ranging from the timely addition of soil amendments to composting to strategic cropping.

Crop time frames – Know the first and last planting dates for a wide variety of crops, which increasingly need to be based on local experience rather than on established wisdom.

Plant much earlier and later – Farmers usually rely on conventional planting dates like the LSF (last spring frost) and miss out on early and late production of many produce items. Also, many farmers have inconsistent production and lack any produce to harvest for long periods during the growing season. As a corps member, you need to emphasize very early and late production of crops such as arugula, baby leaf greens, chard, green garlic, lettuce, radish, rhubarb, salad mix, scallion and spinach. You need to be aware of frost tolerance of certain crops to know which ones can be planted beyond the traditional planting dates.

Season Extension Optional – Know that SPIN-Farming is not based on season extension. Season extension increases the challenge of a start-up operation, and it is recommended that farmers incorporate this into their operations only after they have mastered the basics.

Marketing Weeks – Know that SPIN is based on 20 -30 marketing weeks, which is the time period for which a farmer aims to have a consistent supply of a wide variety of crops for sale or delivery.

Steady, consistent production – Know how to use SPIN's relay cropping strategy to produce a steady supply of a wide variety of crops throughout the season to produce steady cashflow.

Steady, consistent cashflow – Know how to use SPIN's revenue targeting formula to plan a steady, dependable cash flow throughout the entire season.

Questions to answer:

1. What materials do you need to construct a bed?
2. What are some tools you might use for bed preparation?
3. What are the pro's and con's of a raised bed, and one that is not raised?
4. How do many timely plantings increase production?
5. List some cold hardy crops that can be planted early in the spring.
6. List some late season crops that can survive freezing temperatures.
7. Describe the key concepts of SPIN-Farming's production system and how to generate steady revenue.

Resources

SPIN-Farming® Basics – guide #4, Key Concepts

Extension service and local agriculture departments

Farmer's markets

Your favorite farming books, magazines, and websites

Sustainable and organic farming organizations

Exercises:

❏ Outline the different bed layouts and identify which are suitable to which crops, and how to construct each

❏ Create a crop timeframe table for your area

❏ Implement a production plan that provides a steady supply of vegetables for the longest period of time

❏ Choose a specific size land base and devise a production plan to generate a specific revenue target; for example, 10,000 square feet and $25,000

Efficiency is a key consideration, and this is dictated by work rate.

Marching order #5:

Make farmers efficient with work flow management

The one word we hear most from beginning farmers is "overwhelmed." That's because there is no such thing as specialization; on a small farm, the farmer does it all – planning, seed ordering, planting, harvesting, processing, weeding, watering, pest management, selling, recordkeeping, financial management. SPIN farms are no different. An important component of the SPIN-Farming system is work flow management which is the creation of a weekly plan to schedule each farming task so that no one task becomes overwhelming. Efficiency is a key consideration, and this is dictated by work rate. How long does it take for a single person to make a bed, using different tools? How long does it take to plant a bed or a segment to a certain crop? When will the work be done? How much time per week should be allotted to each task? What does a weekly work flow schedule look like? As a SPIN Corps member you need to help aspiring farmers understand that farming is not a job, it is small business ownership, and that being your own boss requires being an effective manager.

Questions to answer:

1. What is work rate?

2. What are the typical farming tasks that need to be performed weekly?

3. How much time does it take to perform farming tasks, based on your experience?

Resources
SPIN-Farming® Basics - guide #6 on work flow practices
Digging Deeper #1: Work flow (in the SPIN-Farming online learning series)
Develop your own list of work rates for typical farm tasks, using a stopwatch

Exercise:

❑ Show by example how to get all the variety of farming tasks done in the minimal amount of time with a manageable amount of effort

Marching order #6:

Help farmers turn harvesting into a five-days-a-week practice

The most stressful task of any farm operation is harvesting. That is because crops don't wait. When they are ready, they have to be gotten out of the ground. Many beginning farmers fail because they don't have well-established harvesting and post-harvesting protocols. The harvests gang all up at once, the farmer becomes overwhelmed, loses control of the operation, burns out and gives up.

SPIN-Farming's well-thought out five-days-a week harvesting schedule in which a crop or different crops are harvested and processed every day throughout the week keeps a farmer in control of their operation and evens out labor needs. That is the point behind SPIN's high-road harvesting, which requires the investment in a commercial cooler. Commercial refrigeration is key to implementing five day-a-week harvesting because it allows a farmer to store the harvested produce until market day. Cooling produce quickly after it is harvested locks in its nutrition, appearance and taste, and prolongs its shelf life, which, in turn, supports premium pricing. It also allows a farmer to bring much more to market than if they limited their harvesting to just the day before.

> Commercial refrigeration is key to implementing five day-a- week harvesting…

Questions to answer:

1. Why is a five day harvesting work week important?

2. What is the one piece of equipment that is needed to practice the five day-a-week harvesting?

Resources
SPIN-Farming® Basics - guide #6 on work flow practices

Digging Deeper # 1: Work flow
(in the SPIN-Farming online learning series)

Exercises:

❏ Show how harvesting, washing and prepping produce can be done efficiently

❏ Develop a sample harvesting schedule for a week, including time estimates and types and amounts of crops harvested

❏ Establish your own work rates for harvesting tasks

Marching order #7:

Help farmers start affordably with SPIN's signature investments
The SPIN-Farming business model replaces capital with labor. So while it is low capital intensive, it is highly labor intensive. This trade-off is readily apparent in the type of investments that are required. Most of the labor relies on standard garden-grade hand tools, though a few specialty tools, like a seeder, collinear hoe, stirrup hoe and wheel hoe, aren't typically found in the shed of most home gardeners. These tools reduce the amount of hand work by 80 – 90% and decrease the time it takes to plant and weed from hours to minutes. A seeder costs about $200, while the specialty hoes cost about $100 each. If properly maintained, these tools are one-time investments. The only mechanized tool equipment that is used is a rototiller. This can be purchased used for about $1,500. A top-of–the line new one costs about $5,000 and will provide many years of service.

Many SPIN farmers use their personal vehicle as their farm vehicle, thereby eliminating this expense entirely.

Another important investment is irrigation, and again, most of the equipment used is standard garden-grade hoses, drip tape and attachments. Different plots are set up using different types of irrigation, depending on the crop grown. This type of Irrigation system is extremely water efficient and economical, ranging in cost from a few hundred to a few thousand dollars, depending on the size of operation.

The most important investment required is a commercial cooler. As pointed out previously, commercial refrigeration capacity is key to taking the high-road because it locks in the value of harvested produce and allows SPIN farmers to practice five days-a-week harvesting. For SPIN farmers the optimal size of a commercial cooler is about 8 feet by 8 feet. Costs can range from $3,000 for a used one up to $10,000 for a new one, and they can be bought from a commercial refrigeration supplier which also handles the installation.

An upright produce cooler, like the ones used in convenience stores, is a more economical option. It measures about 6 feet high, 4 feet wide and 40 inches deep and can frequently be bought at bankruptcy sales for under $1,000. The advantage to an upright cooler is that it plugs into a standard wall outlet, and it is modular so additional coolers can be purchased as a farm operation expands. For those who are handy, do-it-yourself systems like the Coolbot, are another option.

A post-harvesting station and shed are the only farm infrastructure investments. A well-designed post-harvesting station need not be elaborate, expensive or even permanent. What is needed is adequate work space that is sheltered and easily cleaned. Ideally it should be located close to the plots, water source and cooler to minimize the distance from plot to cooler. Minimally, it can consist of an outside patio area with a few picnic tables, beach umbrellas for shade and a few wash bins. Wash water can be reused on the farm plots, and all organic waste can be composted. A SPIN farmer can spend as little or as much as they can afford, with the cost ranging from hundreds to a few thousand dollars. A shed, too, can cost a little or a lot. If a farmer has a spare corner of a garage, they can eliminate this cost entirely.

Most SPIN farmers start their careers selling at farmer's markets so a farm stand is another piece of standard operating equipment. A canopy is the most expensive component of a farm stand, costing in the $300 range. Tables, tablecloths, baskets or bins are all modest expenses. Signs can be made very inexpensively on a computer or at a local print shop.

One of the largest investments a SPIN farmer may need to make is in a delivery vehicle, but because of their sub-acre scale, it does not need to be a semi or half ton truck. Instead, a mini-van, cargo van or even an SUV can accommodate most farming needs. Many SPIN farmers use their personal vehicle as their farm vehicle, thereby eliminating this expense entirely.

Another possible investment that could be a considerable expense is fencing. Those who are rurally-based need to keep out four legged pests, and those in urban or suburban areas need to guard against two legged ones. Chain link fencing is the most secure and the most expensive, though it can be pressed into service as growing space. To fence a half-acre can cost as much as $18,000. Less expensive alternatives include chicken wire.

As seen above, the total amount necessary to start up a sub-acre SPIN farm is a fraction of that of a larger scale farm. Depending on resources and the scale of the operation, a SPIN start-up budget can range from the high three figures to the mid-five figures. Creating a SPIN farm is much less expensive than creating a conventional farm or a typical franchise operation.

Creating a SPIN farm is much less expensive than creating a conventional farm…

Questions to answer:

1. What is the importance of investing in a produce cooler?
2. What are all the other SPIN-Farming investments?

Resources

SPIN-Farming® Basics - guide #3, Investments and Operating Models

Commercial refrigeration supply companies

Garden supply catalogs

Local hardware store for irrigation components

Local garden centers for tools and equipment

Exercises:

❏ Source out local suppliers of commercial refrigeration and DIY yourself refrigeration
❏ Find sources for specialty garden tools like seeders, collinear and stirrup hoes, and cultivators
❏ Describe how an irrigation system is created
❏ Find sources of common garden tools and equipment
❏ Find dealers for new and used rototillers
❏ Determine options and costs for fencing
❏ Create a start-up budget for a 5,000 square foot backyard-based farm

…getting good prices is more in a farmer's control than they are used to thinking…

Marching order #8:

Sell farmers on direct marketing and innovative pricing

It is a cliche that most farmers are great at growing, but they are failures at properly valuing and selling their crops, and as a result they barely eke out a living. This is not a great tradition to be upholding, and in fact, much of the farming industry's revitalization depends on establishing direct customer connections. For a farmer, this has several advantages. The prime one is financial. By eliminating the middle man, a farmer keeps 100% of their sales. Direct marketing sales channels include farmers markets, restaurants, Community Supported Agriculture programs and buying clubs. More details on how these fit into SPIN-Farming marketing, as well as alternatives for new farmers who may not have access to farmers markets, will be provided when you are accepted into the corps program.

Direct marketing also supports higher pricing because farmers can turn the story of the food into economic worth in the marketplace. This is the essence of the SPIN-Farming business model - a SPIN farmer's "value-add" is passing along their knowledge of their crops and how to use them. While being able to put a face to the food carries a price, good prices don't just happen by a farmer showing up. To generate a good income, SPIN farmers need to devise innovative pricing strategies . One example of innovative pricing is SPIN's mix-and-match multiple unit pricing which offers a variety of produce items at the same price tier.

An example is $3.00 per item, or any two for $5.00. This price tier might include 1/4 lb. bags of spinach, large onion bunches, radish bunches, and 1/2 lb. bags of lettuce heads, all at the same price. With this type of unit pricing, a customer knows exactly what they are going to get for $5.00, and they usually look forward to considering their choices. This encourages customers to spend more money since they are not focused on per pound pricing, and it also makes farm stand shopping a more pleasant experience. Farmers who use loose produce pricing, meaning that customers pick loose produce from a bin, often have slow processing times, and many times lines form at their stands. Customers can get impatient and some have limited amounts of time, and farmers can lose sales because of this.

Multiple price tier pricing is another effective technique. In one case there might be items priced at $2, or any 3 items for $4. These are on a separate table from items priced at $4.00 per item, or any 3 for $10. Multiple unit pricing is a highly engaged form of pricing which requires farmers to explain it as potential customers come by. It is a way to "break the ice" with them, and once it is explained, it quickly breaks down customer resistance to making a purchase.

The important point is that getting good prices is more in a farmer's control than they are used to thinking, and they should never take pricing as something that is fixed. Prices should vary according to the volume of production, demand and market conditions. Crops can carry higher pricing early in the season, or if supplies are tight. Pricing can't be an afterthought or taken for granted, and innovative pricing systems will translate into better sales.

Questions to answer:

1. What are examples of some direct marketing sales channels?

2. What is a SPIN farmer's unique selling proposition?

3. How does SPIN's mix-and-match multiple unit pricing work?

Resources
SPIN-Farming® Basics - guide #7, Marketing
Your local farmers market
Business and food reporters for local publications and websites

Exercises:

❑ Assess the demand for local food in your area

❑ Visit a farmer's market and do a survey of crops that are most and least available, and comparative prices

❑ Develop an innovative pricing scheme and explain its rationale

Be part of something that offers the benefits of a franchise without the cost, complications and conformity. »

Photo courtesy of Linda Borghi, Abundant Life Farm

Join the SPIN Corps!

Section 1: What You Are Joining
Section 2: Your Marching Orders

Section 3: How You Make Money
Serving a need…Promoting yourself…Product #1: SPIN-Farming guides…Product #2: SPIN-Farming workshops…Product #3: SPIN-Farming online support…Special bonus – Good times and fellowship…Are you ready?…Looking ahead

Afterwords
Lexicon
Frequently Asked Questions

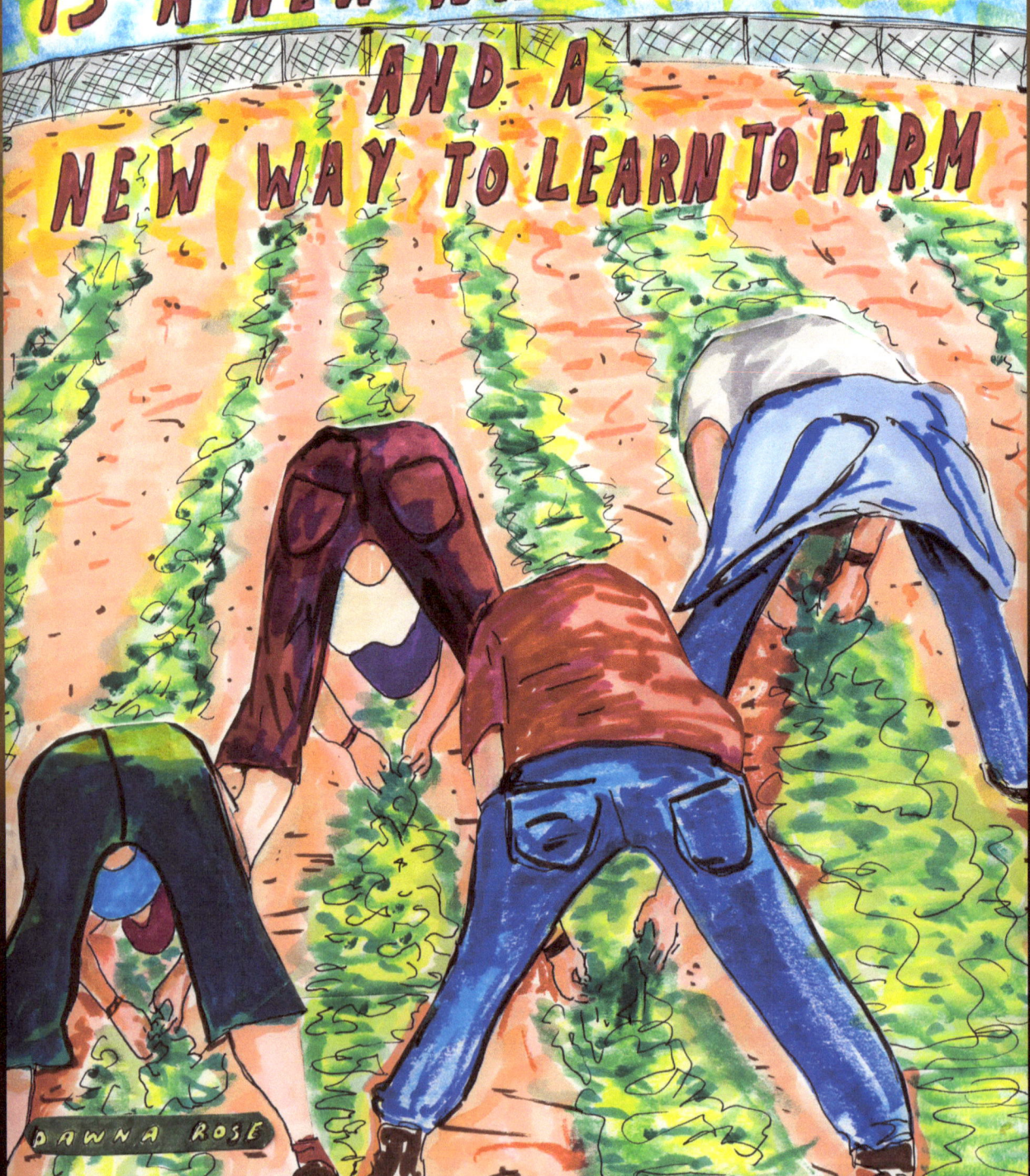

SECTION 3: How You Make Money

...a point that has gotten lost amid all the zeal to reconnect with the source of our food is that farming is an occupation.

Serving a need

Now that you know what's involved in understanding and communicating what SPIN-Farming is, let's define the need you are serving. Farming has a long oral tradition, with knowledge being passed down from generation to generation. But that approach no longer works because 1) at least one or two generations have opted out of the farming profession, so there is a lack of sufficient mentors and 2) the type of farming that is being practiced has not kept up with the times, so that much of the knowledge base that is available is out-of-touch with current economic and cultural realities. SPIN-Farming is not only a new way to farm. It's a new way to learn to farm.

When Farmville, the online game, has over 700,000 players, you know there is significant interest in farming. Mainstream media has adopted farming as its latest cause du jour. There is even a national magazine devoted entirely to urban farming. Your challenge will not be in attracting interest, but in qualifying it. Much of it is being driven by advocates who take pleasure in food growing as part of a lifestyle, or activists who hold strong opinions about the negative effects of our industrial food system.

Ironically, a point that has gotten lost amid all the zeal to reconnect with the source of our food is that farming is an occupation. It not only takes passion. It requires talent, commitment, training, knowledge and business savvy. It is no different than any other highly-skilled profession. The mission of SPIN-Farming, and the need you will be serving, is to provide professional development for the non-traditional aspiring farmer, someone who has not necessarily grown up connected to the land, and who is approaching farming primarily as a business. This non-traditional farmer can be anyone, anywhere, and there are no doubt many in your region eager to get started, if they only knew how. You as the local SPIN-Farming representative are the answer to their dreams, prayers and ambitions, and as such your job will be very easy once these people find you. The task for you is to be sure they do.

Promoting yourself

To promote SPIN-Farming you basically have to promote yourself. There are a variety of no-cost or low-cost ways to do this, and you will be provided with a self-promotion check list when you are accepted into the SPIN Corps program.

For the first time in history the vast majority of tomorrow's farmers will have to come from non-farming backgrounds.

In addition to your SPIN-Farming expertise, the most valuable asset you have as a SPIN Corps member is your connection to the worldwide SPIN community, which contains some of the brightest and most innovative minds in farming today. You can provide that connection to others via the SPIN farmers peer-to-peer online support group. If you are a member yourself, (and if not, you will be required to be one if you become a SPIN Corps member), you know the collective wisdom and experience that is shared there is invaluable, especially to new farmers who have questions on everything from "How do I prep my soil?" to "What temperature should I keep my cooler at?" to "What are some packaging ideas and price points for salad dressings?"

Being able to tap into the expertise of practicing SPIN farmers is like having hundreds of mentors standing by to offer advice and encouragement. And because support group membership is invitation-only, the quality of the discussions remains high and on-point, unlike other farming or gardening forums which often devolve into philosophical debates or explaining gardening basics.

As a corps member, you have the ability to offer free membership into the SPIN online support group, and this is a powerful incentive for new farmers to seek you out. To arrange their membership, all you need to do is provide us with the names and email addresses of those you determine to be worthy group members based on their seriousness of purpose, and they will be emailed an invitation to join the group free, with your compliments. Once word starts getting around that you are the local go-to person for SPIN-Farming, here is what you have to sell.

Product #1: SPIN-Farming Guides

Your core product will be the SPIN guides. Print copies of both *SPIN-Farming® Basics* and *SPIN-Farming 2.0: Produtiron Planning & Crop Profiles* can be ordered online through our on-demand printer and fulfillment house. You use your reseller discount code to purchase book copies as you need them on a non-refundable basis. New guides are always in development so your product line will grow along with the SPIN-Farming learning series. Reseller terms, pricing guidelines and procedures will be provided when you apply to the corps program.

Product #2: SPIN-Farming Workshops

At this moment many countries, and especially the US and Canada, are entering unchartered territory when it comes to farming and new farmer training. For the first time in history the vast majority of tomorrow's farmers will have to come from non-farming backgrounds. City folks will have to be trained to become farm folks because there simply aren't enough farm kids out there to meet the demand, which is growing exponentially and is concentrated in cities. This represents tremendous opportunity for you as a SPIN Corps member. In fact, you probably have your life's work cut out for you. You will be training and mentoring a whole new generation of farmers. Pricing and revenue potential for workshops will be explained when you apply to the corps program.

Once you become accepted into the corps program, we'll provide you with content for a one day SPIN-Farming workshop which you can expand to reflect you own farming experience and speaking style. We, or a fellow corps member, will help you rehearse your presentation, and you will be provided a check list on workshop logistics, pricing and marketing.

A network of fellow career farmers is an important support mechanism…

Product # 3: SPIN-Farming Online Support

The most profitable product in farming is knowledge, and farmers have been giving that away, in random bits and pieces, for years. As you know by now, that is not the SPIN way. SPIN farmers value their expertise as highly as they do their golden purslane and Mokum carrots. The SPIN Corps gives them a way to share and profit from their know-how by participating in SPIN-Farming Online Support. Here's how it works.

Based on the type of guidance farmers have sought from us over the years, we have developed a series of simple, one page diagnostics on such topics as underperforming famer's market sales, and initial start-up farm design,. We provide these to corps members to sell via their websites or email lists. Their customers complete and return the diagnostic to the corps member who then offers advice and recommendations by return email.

If any of the challenges a corps member receives is beyond his or her area of expertise, they email fellow corps members for additional input. The collective and individual knowledge of the group grows along with each corps members business and revenue. Over time, corps members will develop and contribute new diagnostics in areas they know a lot about to build out the online support repertoire. Think of it as a way to structure and share the collective knowledge and wisdom of SPIN farmers. It is a co-op that sells knowledge instead of crops, with SPIN-Farming providing the platform and the brand.

So just as SPIN-Farming makes agricultural education affordable and accessible to anyone, anywhere, SPIN-Farming Online Support does the same for farm mentoring. You will be provided specifics on how you can participate in SPIN-Farming Online Support when you are accepted into the SPIN Corps program.

Special Bonus – Good Times and Fellowship

In addition to being overwhelmed, the challenge we hear most from beginning farmers, especially in urban and suburban areas, is isolation. This is not surprising given that the number of professional farmers has declined dramatically for the past two generations, and that farming inside cities and towns is still somewhat of a novelty. A network of fellow career farmers is an important support mechanism, and while the online SPIN group is a source for broad-based knowledge and perspectives, it cannot provide highly-specific, "on the ground" advice and guidance. Creating a way, either formal or informal, for local SPIN farmers to meet face-to-face to share tips and challenges is a big opportunity for you as a corps member. You can be as ambitious as your time and resources allow, and there is no one-size-fits-all approach that can be dictated. You need to determine what's best based on the needs and interests of the community of farmers you are helping to build, but fellowship and good times are sure to follow.

Are You Ready?

Now that you know what is involved in becoming a corps member, the question for you to answer is, "Are you ready to grow more than just crops?" If you want to grow a business based on providing learning and opportunity for others, the SPIN Corps wants you! There is no fee to apply, and the process is straightforward. It starts, as many great collaborations do, by contacting us online at the SPIN-Farming website – www.spinfarming.com – and asking for an application.

Looking Ahead

As you know, SPIN farmers are always looking ahead, and we are here to support their visions. As usually happens with SPIN, those who embrace it discover talents they did not know they had. So what may very well happen is that, once you become a corps member you'll discover you're a great teacher, and you'll want to start an official SPIN training center to produce additional business beyond your immediate geographical area, as well as offering SPIN advanced courses. Or maybe you find you're a good host, and you'll want to become an events manager by organizing an annual SPIN festival. Whatever the future holds for you, we're open to supporting whatever s-mall p-lot in-spirations come your way.

"The highly productive home gardens of tomorrow will, I think,
be the sprouts from which many new small farms will grow. The
small-scale farmers of the future can hardly learn their craft
in the land-grant colleges, which preach bigness in almost
every way. These new farmers will start as gardeners and grow
from there. I think that we will see the size of gardens
increase, so that the distinction between a large garden and
a small farm will become blurred. The new wave of small farms
will fill in the chinks of land made available as some of the
old-style farmers are driven out of business by ever-bigger
farming conglomerates."

– Robert Rodale, Rodale Institute, Emmaus PA, 1990

Help people realize what is possible and do what is practical. »

Join the SPIN Corps!

Afterwords

Lexicon
Frequently Asked Questions

SPIN FARMING® Lexicon

SPIN-Farming has its own unique techniques and language. To help get your head around how SPIN differs from conventional farming methods, or from home gardening, here's a translation of the important terms you'll be using as a SPIN Corps member.

Sub-acre land base – SPIN transfers commercial farming techniques to sub-acre land bases. Farmers do not need to own much, or any land, to start their operations, and they can be single or multi-sited.

Structured work flow practices – SPIN outlines a deliberate and disciplined day-by-day work routine so that the wide variety of farm tasks can be easily managed without any one task becoming overwhelming.

High-road/Low-road – SPIN distinguishes between two different harvesting techniques. High-road utilizes commercial refrigeration equipment. Low-road harvesting does not.

High-value crops – SPIN devotes most of its land base to the production of high-value crops, defined as ones that generate at least $100 per crop/per bed.

Relay cropping – SPIN calls for the sequential growing of crops in a single bed throughout a single season.

Intensive relays – 3 or 4 crops per season are grown.

Bi-relays – 2 crops per bed per season are grown.

Single crops – 1 crop per bed per season is grown.

1-2-3 bed layout – Refers to the 3 different areas of a SPIN farm devoted to the different levels of production intensity.

75/25 land allocation – Dictates how much land is assigned to the different levels of production on a SPIN farm. The aim is to balance production between high-value and low-value crops to produce a steady revenue stream and to target revenue based on farm size. The smaller the land base the more of it can be devoted to intensive relay production.

Farm layout – SPIN provides guidelines for segmenting a land base into a series of beds, separated by access alleys, which are small 2 feet strips, just wide enough for a rototiller. An acre accommodates approximately 480 standard size beds, including the necessary paths and access alleys. SPIN can also incorporate more traditional approaches to land allocation.

Standard size beds – SPIN utilizes beds measuring 2 feet wide by 25 feet long.

Revenue targeting formula – By growing high-value crops worth $100 per harvest per bed, and by practicing intensive relay cropping which produces at least 3 crops per bed per season, SPIN targets at least $300 in gross sales per bed per season. With approximately 480 beds per acre, the maximum revenue potential is 480 beds x $300 per bed per season = $144,000 gross sales per acre. When farming is approached in terms of beds instead of acres, the result is a very precise idea of how much growing space can be utilized, and how that space can be managed to generate predictable and steady income.

Organic-based – SPIN relies on all-organic farming practices. There are minimal off-farm inputs and very little waste.

Crop Diversity – A SPIN product line contains a very wide diversity of crops, with some SPIN farms producing over 100 different varieties and 50 different types of crops per season. However, SPIN also provides models that specialize in a particular crop.

Season extension is optional – SPIN does not rely on season extension to expand production; however season extension can be utilized to push SPIN yields and income significantly higher.

Direct marketing – SPIN bases crop selection on what local markets want. Being close to markets allows for constant product feedback and ensures a loyal and dependable customer base. Grow what you sell, don't sell what you grow, is the SPIN farmer's mantra.

Mix and match multiple unit pricing – SPIN's marketing approach is to pre-bag produce items and sell them at certain price tiers – for example, $3.00/unit or any 2 for $5.00.

Commercial refrigeration capacity – SPIN calls for taking the "high-road" by utilizing commercial refrigeration capacity because cooling crops immediately after they are harvested retains their quality which supports premium pricing. It also provides control over the harvest schedule and allows for a manageable work flow.

Minimal mechanization and infrastructure – SPIN's most important and costly equipment are a rototiller and a walk-in cooler or upright produce cooler. All other SPIN implements and infrastructure can be sourced at local garden supply or hardware stores.

"Home-based" work crew – Supplemental labor requirements for a SPIN farm are minimal and can be readily obtained within the network of family, friends, or within the local community.

Utilization of existing water sources – SPIN relies on local water service or wells for all of its irrigation needs.

Low capital intensive – Minimal infrastructure and minimal overhead keeps SPIN farm's start-up and operating expenses manageable. The bottom line is little or no debt.

"If you look into history, what the early settlers of America were for a large part trying to accomplish, was to escape the clutches of the European central bankers and set up a self-reliant society that didn't need the money and debt from the central bankers. I find that today we are in the exact same situation, except that there are no new islands or continents to discover where we can start a new society. Instead, we have to do it in our own communities, cities, provinces, states and countries. Commercial farming allows you to free yourself from whatever career or job you may have been locked into before, and truly "walk the talk" of social change. Not just be a weekend warrior, and talk about change on the weekends, but then check your values at the door, when you go to work. For people who come from a mid to lower class income like myself, SPIN-Farming is a methodology on how to earn a living from land you don't own. How much more accessible could that be? I have said this many times: the revolution has to be funded by the revolution."

– Curtis Stone, owner/operator, Green City Acres, Kelowna, BC, 2012

Help people see the world through SPIN glasses »

Photo courtesy of John Yovetich, John's Backyard Garden

Join the SPIN Corps!

Afterwords

Lexicon
Frequently Asked Questions

Frequently Asked Questions

As the local go-to person on SPIN-Farming you'll be fielding lots of questions. To help prepare you, here are answers to questions we have been asked the most since we began pioneering sub-acre farming practices in 2006. Some are posed by aspiring farmers short on cash or land or both. Some come from concerned citizens looking to make their communities more farm-friendly. Others are asked by reporters who know a good story when they see one. Still others are asked by policymakers who are realizing that sustainability is more than just an egghead phrase. If you ever get stumped, your fellow SPIN Corps members are standing by...

Can the average person do SPIN-Farming?

As near as we can tell, success at SPIN-Farming or any other kind of farming, is not determined by education level or prior work experience. What you do need is a deep and passionate interest in farming, which involves working outside long hours in all kinds of weather (some have described it as a calling to farm), a genuine talent for growing, a good business sense, and a willingness to invest years in learning, training and building a business. If you have all that, SPIN-Farming makes it easier and less risky to get started and increases your chances of success.

Can SPIN-Farming turn a brown thumb into a green thumb?

No. If you haven't met a plant you can't kill, farming is not your line of work.

What are SPIN-Farming's margins?

Farming is not like a grocery store, which buys produce and resells it at a markup. With entrepreneurial farming, it's more helpful to think of yearly overhead, or expenses. The SPIN-Farming system provides ways to reduce expenses because of its sub-acre scale. Examples include using your personal vehicle as a farm vehicle; creating an inexpensive irrigation system from standard grade garden hoses; minimal mechanization; organic-based, local sources of supply for fertilizer; an inexpensive post-harvesting setup; and minimizing or even eliminating the need for outside labor, which is the single biggest expense of any farm operation.

How many hours per week does a SPIN farmer work?

SPIN-Farming is not based on season extension, so most operations span about 8 months.
In the SPIN hobby farm model, during peak season, which is mid-summer for most, a farmer will put in 40 - 45 hours each week, spread out over 7 days. During non-peak months, the number of hours drop to about 30 hours each week, spread out over 7 days. In a SPIN full-time half-acre farm model, during peak season, a farmer couple will each put in 40 - 45 hours each week, spread out over 7 days. They may have occasional outside help. During non-peak months, the number of hours will be about 30 hours each week, spread out over 7 days.

In a SPIN full-time 1 acre farm model, during peak season a farmer couple will each be putting in about 50 - 60 hours each week, spread out over 7 days. They may have occasional outside help. During non-peak months, the number of hours will be about 35 hours each week, spread out over 7 days.

How much land should I initially put into production?

SPIN-Farming is based on allocating your land base to different areas of production intensity. The system is based on the 1-2-3 layout, where the 1 area of your farm is the least intensive and is devoted to lower value single crops per season, like cabbage, onion, potatoes or squash. The 2 area of your farm is devoted to bi-relay crops, in which 2 higher-value crops per bed per season are grown sequentially. And the 3 area of your farm is where you are doing your intensive relays in which 3 or more high-value crops per bed per season are grown sequentially. Each of these areas contribute a different amount to your total income, with the 3 high-value area obviously contributing the most.

SPIN-Farming is an exercise in figuring out how much money you want to make, determining the amount of your operation that needs to be put in the most intensive form of production to generate that income, and the labor needed to support that. This is not figured out in one season. It takes years of experience to find the optimum balance.

You can't reinvent farming. What is so new about SPIN?

We agree that many of farming's best practices date back quite a ways and don't need improvement. But much of the current disconnect about food is due to the geographical separation between where we grow it and where we live and work. In an increasingly urbanized world, segregating food production outside of cities and towns no longer makes sense, so the scale of commercial farming has to adapt to become compatible with densely populated areas. Because SPIN-Farming greatly reduces the amount of land needed for commercial crop production, it integrates farming into the built environment without conflict. It thereby allows farmers to locate close to their markets and converts otherwise vacant or underutilized land to productive use.

Why does SPIN-Farming make business sense?

There are three reasons why SPIN makes good business sense:
First, as noted above, SPIN allows for farmers to market direct to their customers, which eliminates the middleman and allows a farmer to keep 100% of his/her sales.

Second, SPIN removes the 2 big barriers to entry for new farmers - land and capital.

Third, SPIN increases reduces a farmer's expenses Examples of lower expenses in the SPIN-Farming system include: using a personal vehicle as a farm vehicle - a mini or cargo van or mini-truck is adequate in size for sub-acre scale farming; creating an inexpensive irrigation system from standard grade garden hoses; using minimal mechanization - no expensive equipment is necessary; using organic-based, local sources of supply for fertilizer which eliminates the use of expensive chemicals; using an inexpensive post-harvesting setup; and minimizing or even eliminating the need for outside labor, which is the single biggest expense of any farm operation.

The aim with SPIN-Farming is to keep expenses at 10% to 20% of total sales. So if you target $50,000 in sales then you should target $5,000 to $10,000 in expenses. The high end would account for some hired labor. Labor is the single biggest expense in any farm operation, so SPIN farmers aim to minimize or even eliminate the need for outside labor. It very much carries on the tradition of conventional farming of tapping into the low-cost, no-cost network of family and friends and barters labor for produce when possible.

Doesn't SPIN's intensive growing techniques deplete the soil?

Intensive relay cropping will give your soil a workout, but because of the sub-acre scale of SPIN-Farming, it is much easier to keep your soil healthy, and at a reasonable cost. You can use your rototiller to plow in compost, and individual beds can be amended on a case-by-case basis. Locally-sourced, all organic amendments can be used that would not be feasible on larger scale farms. Many of these amendments are available at local animal feed stores in 50 pound bags, and they are not laborious to apply.

Many of the crops in SPIN's intensive relays are not heavy feeders, and even though you are growing 3 or more crops per bed per growing season in the intensive relay area, the demands on the soil are not as great as some single long season crops such as corn. When growing crops in the relay area you often do so in a series. For instance you might have a section where you have 10 beds of carrots. Carrots, in fact, do not like an overly fertile soil, so you need not go on a "fertilizing binge" prior to planting. Also, some relay crops are nitrogen fixers, such as beans and peas.

So although the relay areas see a lot of production, burning out your soil can be avoided with modest soil amendments and strategic planting. Just follow the guideline that "inputs need to equal outputs" and amend on an ongoing basis by lightly fertilizing after each crop, as well as side dressing long season crops, especially garlic. Again, keep in mind that some crops, such as carrots, lettuce, radish and fresh herbs, are light feeders while others, such as spinach, garlic, onions and beets are heavier feeders, and adjust your amending appropriately.

What impact will the economic downturn have on SPIN farmers?

The economic downturn will have impact in three areas of relevance to SPIN farmers:

Sustainability – Now that we have seen the consequences of a financial system that is unsustainable, sustainability has more currency and legitimacy. It is no longer just an abstract, moral imperative, and it is spurring permanent changes in how our country operates. This can only help SPIN and other farm systems that are based on sound economic and environmental practices.

Entrepreneurship – Establishing independent businesses will be more attractive since incentives for joining the corporate system have been undermined or removed. Striking out on your own carries less risk than it used to, and some of this unleashed new entrepreneurship can be channeled into farming.

Staying put – For many, the costs and disruption of mobility have become too much to bear. So value will be shifted closer to home, resulting in re-investment in local communities. Economics will become more place-based, and this will help the re-establishment of more locally-based food systems. Overall, we'd say the future is in the SPIN farmer's favor.

What is urban agriculture?

Because SPIN's efforts have been focused on providing a business case for urban agriculture, we define it as integrating agriculture into the built environment in an economically viable manner

Where is my city on the urban ag adoption curve?

At this point, there is no curve. Just about every city is starting from square one when it comes to developing agricultural self-sufficiency. So the good news is no one is late to the party or too far ahead of the curve, but the bad news is there is no set of best practices or implementation plan that can be plugged in and followed. Ever city is making it up as they go along. None of them want to re-invent the wheel and seek out models that they can replicate, which is what leads them to SPIN-Farming.

We tell cities that we can guarantee they already have 3 of the critical success factors for urban agriculture, and the other 2 are theirs for the asking.

What cities have is land, though they often find this hard to believe. But once they adopt SPIN's sub-acre mindset, they start to see lots of possibilities. Cities also have a variety of easily accessible markets and financing sources for the micro level financing that is all sub-acre farming operations need.

Entrepreneurial farmers are theirs for the asking, as more and more first generation farmers are eager to recast farming as a small business inside cities. Some of these aspiring farmers are native born city dwellers that can be cultivated with the proper training, while others can be attracted from outside cities' borders. The other thing that is theirs for the asking is appropriately scaled farming systems, and SPIN provides one model.

Can SPIN-Farming work in (name any place in the world)?

SPIN is not placed-based. It is currently being practiced throughout the U.S., Canada, Australia, the UK, Ireland, the Netherlands, New Zealand and South Africa. Each SPIN farmer adapts the system to his or her climate, markets, talents and available resources. There are two things all SPIN farmers do have in common – markets to support them, and an entrepreneurial spirit. They are creating their farm businesses without major policy changes or government support. They are highly small plot independent.

Can SPIN work with other growing systems?

SPIN is a production system, not a belief system. It is not predicated on any one set of life principals or philosophy, or any one method of soil prep or maintenance. It can be combined with biointensive, biodynamic, permaculture, vermaculture, acquaponics, double dig, no till. We recommend the use of a rototiller because it increases efficiency which results in high income. But if a rototiller does not fit in with the way you think the world should work, and you are willing to accept the consequences to your bottom line, you can choose not to use it.

So is SPIN a movement?

Ask those who are doing it.

About the Authors

Wally Satzewich

> "We're trying to open up farming to a lot of different people that might not have seen it as possible for them."

Wally Satzewich and Gail Vandersteen operate Wally's Urban Market Garden which is a multi-locational sub-acre urban farm. It was originally dispersed over 25 residential backyard garden plots in Saskatoon, Saskatchewan, that were rented from homeowners. The sites range in size from 500 square feet to 3,000 square feet, and the growing area totals a half-acre. The produce is sold at The Saskatoon Farmers Market and restaurants in the city.

Wally and Gail initially started farming on an acre-size plot outside of Saskatoon 20 years ago. Thinking that expanding acreage was critical to their success, they bought some farmland adjacent to the South Saskatchewan river 40 miles north of Saskatoon where they eventually grew vegetables on about 20 acres of irrigated land. The farmland was considered an idyllic farming site on its riverfront location. However, the crops were perpetually challenged by wind and hail, insect infestation, rodents and deer. Fluctuating water levels inhibited irrigation during dry spells. "We still lived in the city where we had a couple of small plots to grow crops like radishes, green onion and salad mix, which were our most profitable crops. We could grow three crops a year on the same site, pick and process on-site and put the produce into our cooler so it would be fresh for the market," Gail says.

After six years farming their rural site, the couple realized there was more money to be made growing multiple crops intensively in the city, so they sold the farm and became urban growers. Growing vegetable crops in the city was less complicated than mechanized, large-scale farming. They used to have a tractor to hill potatoes and cultivate, but they discovered it's more efficient to do things by hand. Other than a rototiller, all they need is a push-type seeder and a few hand tools.

They have recently expanded their multi-locational vegetable and flower gardens in the hamlet of Pleasantdale, Saskatchewan which will serve as the home base for training programs on sub-acre farming.

Wally points out that urban growing provides a more controlled environment, with fewer pests, better wind protection and a longer growing season. "We are producing 10-15 different crops and sell thousands of bunches of radishes and green onions and thousands of bags of salad greens and carrots each season. Our volumes are low compared to conventional farming, but we sell high-quality organic products at very high-end prices." The SPIN-Farming method is based on Wally's successful experiment in downsizing and emphasizes minimal mechanization and maximum fiscal discipline and planning.

Brian Halweil, a food issues writer and researcher at the Washington-DC-based Worldwatch Institute, interviewed Wally and referenced his farming approach in Eat Here, which documents worldwide initiatives in building locally-based food industries.

About the Authors

Roxanne Christensen

Roxanne Christensen co-founded Somerton Tanks Farm, a half-acre demonstration urban farm that served as the U.S. test bed for the SPIN-Farming method from 2003 to 2006. The farm, which was operated in partnership with the Philadelphia Water Department, received the support of the Pennsylvania Dept. Of Agriculture, the Philadelphia Workforce Development Corp., the City Commerce Department, the USDA Natural Resources Conservation Service, the Pennsylvania Department of Environmental Protection, and the Pennsylvania Department of Community and Economic Development.

"We can't explain GAIA, but we can explain commercial coolers."

In 2003, its first year of operation, the farm, located in the sixth largest city in the U.S, produced $26,000 in gross sales from 20,000 square feet of growing space. In 2006 gross sales reached $68,000. In just four years of operation this demonstration farm achieved levels of productivity and financial success that many agricultural professionals claimed were impossible.

Based on the agricultural and financial breakthroughs that were demonstrated at Somerton Tanks Farm, the state of Pennsylvania funded an economic feasibility study that documented the urban farm's economics and projected its maximum income potential to be $120,000 from under an acre of growing space.

As co-author of the SPIN-Farming online learning series, Roxanne's current role is to attract and support new farming talent. She contends that SPIN-Farming is uniquely suited to entrepreneurs and provides a career path for those who have a calling to farm. It is enticing first generation farmers who are keenly interested in matters of principle, but who understand that to have a significant positive impact, they have to function within the existing system, pushing their cause while paying their bills.

"For aspiring farmers, SPIN-Farming eliminates the 2 big barriers to entry – sizeable acreage and substantial startup capital. At the same time, its intensive relay growing techniques and precise revenue targeting formulas push yields to unprecedented levels and result in highly profitable income," Roxanne says. "While most other farming systems focus primarily if not exclusively on agricultural practices, SPIN-Farming emphasizes the business aspects and provides a financial and management framework for having the business drive the agriculture, rather than the other way around."

As SPIN-Farming becomes established and is practiced more and more widely, Roxanne says, it will create new farmland closer to metropolitan areas, which, in turn will produce environmental, economic and social benefits. "It offers a compelling value proposition."

Photo courtesy of Linda Borghi, Abundant Life Farm

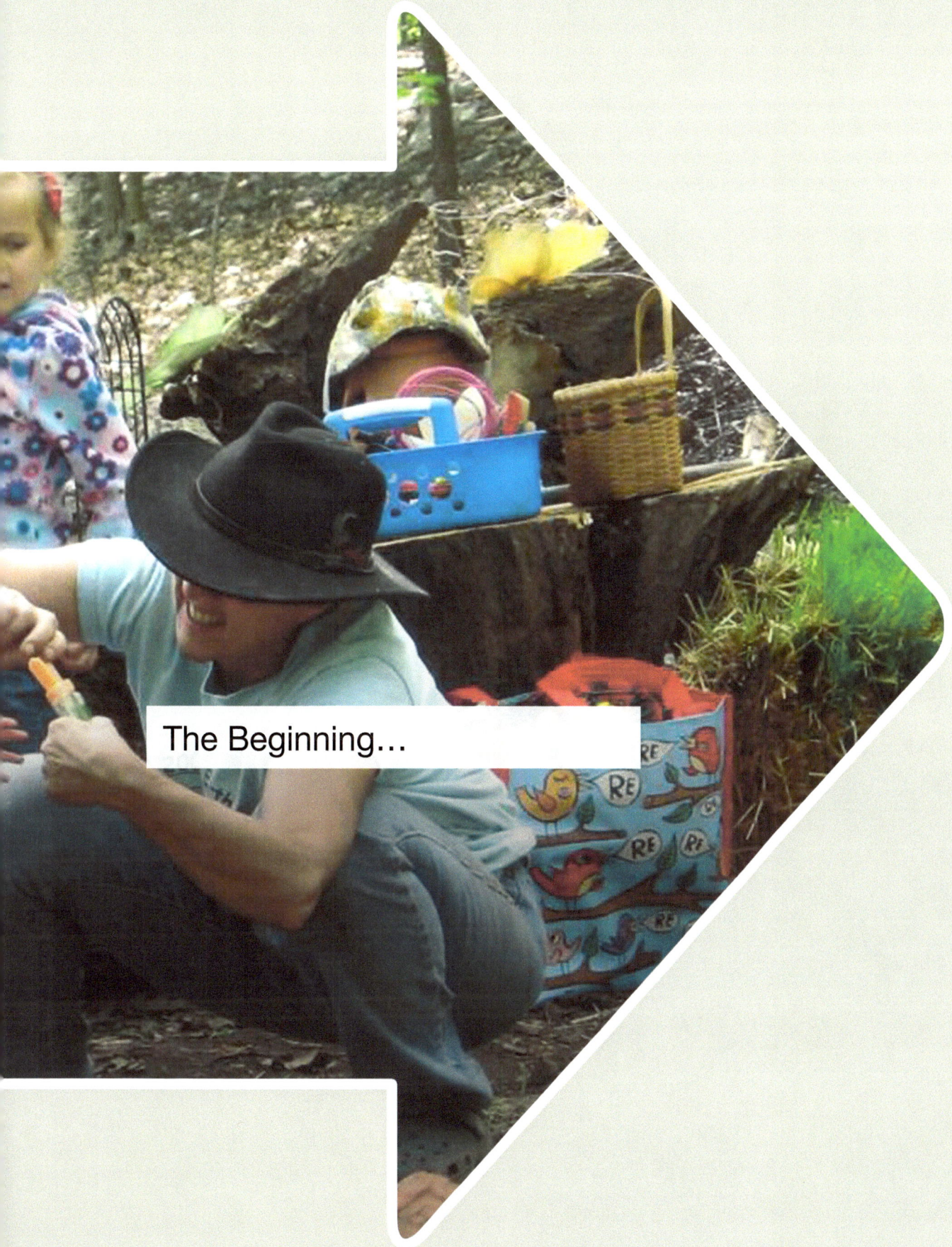

The Beginning…

"Nothing in the world can take the place of persistence. Talent will not; nothing in the world is more common than unsuccessful men with talent. Genius will not; unrewarded genius is almost a proverb. Education will not; the world is full of educated derelicts. Persistence and determination alone are omnipotent."

– Ray Kroc, Chairman, McDonald's Corporation

Photo courtesy of John Yovetich, John's Backyard Garden